Swan Light

Poems by Diane Frank

BLUE LIGHT PRESS ◆ 1ST WORLD PUBLISHING

1ST WORLD
PUBLISHING

SAN FRANCISCO ◆ FAIRFIELD ◆ DELHI

Swan Light

BLUE LIGHT PRESS
www.bluelightpress.com
Email: bluelightpress@aol.com

Book Design and Illustrations:
Melanie Gendron

Cover Art:
"Hummingbird Kiss" by Melanie Gendron

Photograph:
Anders Hansen

Swan Light website:
www.dianefrank.net

FIRST EDITION

LCCN: 2013932520

ISBN: 978-1-4218-8662-6

Praise for Swan Light . . .

"These poems of love returning to love, and light returning to light, are a heart gone supernova. Page by page, Frank burns a path to her readers' hearts. The alignments are profound, the connections electric — from heart to bone, from marrow to star. These are radiant poems, where we earthbound creatures may find simultaneous escape and renewal."
    —George Wallace, Walt Whitman Birthplace Writer in Residence

"There may be those who think of poetry as optional, but Diane Frank's *Swan Light* does not support that thinking, since it addresses a hunger you didn't know you had, first with trace nutrients of the soul, and as you progress, with the solid food of organic experience. Read, savour and be nourished."
    —Paul Stokstad, author of *Butterfly Tattoo*

"In *Swan Light* Diane Frank has written an irrepressible and epic love story: a love story for lover, artist, parent, child, earth, heaven, spirit, body, and music; a love story for what we are forced to leave behind, and for what we are lucky enough to keep; a love story whose thread is the music of love found in the many narratives and lyrics we live while walking, writing, running, dancing, painting, and praying. This is Diane Frank's most ambitious body of poetry to date, and I say "body" because the word "collection" is so inaccurate. This book is a whole, breathing the same breath as the author, and singing a meaning threaded with intricate images and motifs."
    —Rustin Larson, author of *Crazy Star* and *The Wine-Dark House*

"Diane Frank presents in *Swan Light* a finely wrought choreography of poetry that intersects with the music of language and the spirit of dance. In these poems are whole constellations of imagery, a resplendent aurora of words showering down to light up the geography of the page. If poetry should not mean but be, as MacLeish proclaimed, then these poems by Diane Frank truly *are*."
    —Andrena Zawinski, author of *Something About*, PEN Oakland Award

"Here is a book to treasure, to take down frequently for no particular reason, a book to help us remember why we took to poetry in the first place."

—Daniel J. Langton, Creative Writing Program
San Francisco State University

"Diane's poems may seem fanciful at times, but her language belies the truth. Her poems are about survival: finding love and community, creating a lifestyle that embodies art, winnowing the truth from memory. A survival of the soul."

—Stewart Florsheim, author of *The Short Fall from Grace*

"Diane Frank's new book, *Swan Light*, in which "The trees have memories" and "We swim inside / swan light, sky ballet / lifting through the aurora . . ." continues her life-long poetic journey through poignant and nostalgia-inducing images. In this, her latest and best poetry, bears, butterflies, and frogs sprinkle childhood memories and dreams in those universal experiences we all remember (summer camp, prom, moving) via their colorful and sensuous descriptors for which Diane's poetry is known."

—Lynn Cohen, Writing Program, Hofstra University

"Diane's luminous poems are each little symphonies in their own right, buoyant cellular celebrations of supernumerary dimensions yet to unfurl, evocations of deep-time connections perceived yet obliviated within the strange botany of the interpersonal . . . a vibrating and vibrant world that continues to inspire wonder and amazement. I enter the wild fluctuations of her EMF never to leave it: who can fight supergravity? Giving in to the gift of this rush is paradise."

—Michael Angelo Tata, author of *The Multiplication of Joy Into Integers*.

Acknowledgments

Grateful acknowledgment to the following magazines and anthologies in which some of these poems were previously published or accepted for publication:

Blue Unicorn, Sugar Mule, PoetryMagazine.com, Haight Ashbury Literary Journal, Poetrybay, Writing Outside the Lines, Cyclamens and Swords, Albany Poetry Examiner, Conceit Magazine, nebu[lab], Conches, River of Earth and Sky: Poems for the Twenty-First Century, Voices Israel Anthology, Long Island Sounds, This Enduring Gift: A Flowering of Fairfield Poetry, Walt's Corner, Levure Litteraire, Weaving Eucalyptus, Word Landscapes, Majestic Isles Newsletter, Mermaid Dreams, and Shaped by Light and Fog.

"By a Farmhouse in Corvallis" and "Iowa Omen" were printed as broadsides by The Paper Crane for poetry readings at M. Coffee.

"To a Hummingbird" was written for a cello piano duet composed by Erik Ievins and performed by Erik Ievins, cello; and Tom Darter, piano; during a San Francisco Sinfonietta Collage Concert at the Workspace Limited in San Francisco.

"Pool" was set to music by Jan Pusina and performed by Madison Emery Smith, soprano; Erik Ievins, cello; and Carter Scholz, piano, at the Workspace Limited in San Francisco.

"Iowa Omen" and "Finding You" were set to music by Jan Pusina, in a composition called "If. . ." for voice, piano and cello. It will be performed by Kristine Sinajon, Erik Ievins, and a pianist at a San Francisco Sinfonietta Collage concert.

A companion poem to "Dancing in Paradise Café" was written by Paul Stokstad and is published in Butterfly Tattoo by Paul Stokstad (Blue Light Press, San Francisco, 2012).

"Waltz for Young Daughters" was written for music composed by Rebecca King.

Special thanks to Erik Ievins, Jill Brindel, Stephen Dunn, Rustin Larson, Daniel J. Langton, Lynn Cohen, George Wallace, Tammy Nuzzo-Morgan, George James, Lynne Rappaport, Paul Stokstad, David Hurlin, and the Monday Night Poets in Fairfield, Iowa.

In loving memory of my parents,
Irene Frank,
Donald N. Frank and Edith Frank

Contents

DAWN AFTER THE ART WALK

RING OF FIRE

FIRST LIGHT

About the Author

THE SWAN CYCLE

Dancing in Paradise Café

I'm on the floor
with my foot extended to Cassiopeia,
toe pointing to the Pole Star.
I'm twirling into the birth
of a new galaxy,
swirling gasses condensing into the shape
of the choreography of your
left arm
as you pull me into
the salty water of a lunar sea,
where life, against all odds,
is finding its first form.

I dance in a dinosaur's dream,
the edge of a bone,
the heartbeat of a feather
finding the species and genus
of a bird that will fly
into the dance of fingers
exploring the shape of a star
at the apogee
of a dream inside an egg
etched with the wisdom
of an exploding universe.

It's the chanting of an ocean
as it discovers the shape
of a heartbeat
and remembers how to dance,
smoke inside the
breath of the buffalo

running across a primal plain
of first light,
writing on the wall of the cave
where the ocean echoes
into the curve of the penumbra
of a seashell moon.

As you dip me into the Milky Way,
my back is arcing
into the flute's high descant,
singing the memory of the future
where the secret of species is revealed
in the chord of the whir of grasshoppers
on a blue and emerald jewel
in the shape of a double helix,
remembering white fire
in the belt of Orion,
an arrow through time
dreaming the beauty of the Pleiades,
the temple dancer,
her silver bells, her back
a sequence of vectors
across oceans, across time.

By a Farmhouse in Corvallis

His hand is like a hummingbird
difficult to see or freeze frame
at each end of a wide vibrato.

Violin music floating
through a wind tunnel.

We kiss in a hot spring
love each other under the open sky
in shoulder high water,
his eyes radiant as the wings
of a blue heron.

We swim inside
swan light, sky ballet
lifting through the aurora.

Eggshell blue notes, crazy happy,
stolen time.

Letter to Alaska

The full moon is surrounded
by a wide copper ring,
an expanse of light like the halo of a saint.

In the morning,
I am surrounded with eucalyptus
and redwood trees, camellias, calla lilies,
and the swans — mysterious
and astoundingly beautiful creatures.

In my dreams you kiss me.
Your music floats in from Alaska
in streams of aurora borealis.

Inside the aurora
one of my swans floats through —
the cadence of a cello
streaming from the heart,
held inside the holy place,
swan light, sky ballet.

Mendocino Meditation

The trees have memories —
a path in the dark
to a private place we find
over and over again.

Sometimes joy
Sometimes a struggle
Sometimes discordant music waving out
through redwood trees.

Horses of light leaping over the Gualala River,
horses of light inside primary colors.

When my inner light flies away,
gather the meadowlarks
back to my heart.

In the morning, sunlight streaming
through a cacophony of branches,
my struggle, my path
into the great chaos.

Molecules of morning colliding into
a silver dream,
the rhythm of cicadas,
then the voice of the meadowlark
discovering the prelude to the sonata
of first light.

Pool

My words ripple through water.
When they touch you,
you don't understand.
They escape your fingers.

Words surrounded by stones.

Words
          under
                    water.

They swim inside themselves
to find their own light.

In the pool I inhale your skin.
I swim in the scent of you.
My words don't touch you
the way our kisses do.

Our toes touch as
fantail koi brush your skin
in a Japanese temple garden.

My words
swim through the water
push through
the alphabet of your skin.

In the Mendocino Woodlands

He walks into the forest
where trees are burning,
finding his path in the silence.

Woodpecker, memory, larkspur
in the night of burning.

His eyes ask me to wait,
to keep the connection inside
the silent place where I find
pebbles of intuition, rose quartz.

In the morning, lupines on the trail
to the cliff where the giant trillium blooms,
kelp and seals swimming beyond
the tide pools below.

I run through Indian paintbrush,
milkmaids, cinquefoil,
climbing the path where he finds me.

And what is love?
A fire walk initiation
from the ocean through a cathedral of trees,
fuchsia, wild grape, sudden
blue streaks on the wing of a moth,
stellar jay wanting to fly free.

Mendocino Late Night

Walking home through a cathedral
of redwood trees
late night, my body awake
with memories, the blue
of a stellar jay,
the mountain lion we saw
at sunset

Glitter of stars
the voice of wild orchids
A path I find in the dark

High branches
the shape of a rune
Osprey lifting from the Gualala River
What the owl said

An echo of white deer
running to the moon

Sometimes I feel you in the morning
silver koi under the water
of my dream.

Swan Dream

You play piano,
run through shoulder high
fields of summer corn,
disappear inside a wind tunnel.

Sunlight sprays across the room
in feathers of light.

Trills, the silver wings
of a calliope hummingbird
suddenly emerge
in a green rush of feathers
from a hidden place.

It is morning or evening,
a soft pink light
lifting through an expanding sky,
a dance of milky feathers,
a swan swimming through
a streak of rippled water.

Sunlight
makes the walls transparent,
and the sounds of the world
start rushing in.

Percussive

In the forest, two stellar jays
lapis blue.

My heart is a potato chip
snap
                    crunch.

So there you are
down in the depths
looking at the door.

Leap in?
                Run or
step over the moon.

My heart?
A fluttering gypsy moth.

Ariadne

At night you come to me,
dream with me,
make love to me,
teach me where to harmonize
long notes on the cello.

In the morning
I wake up alone
and a small black spider
crawls over my foot
with its message.

The spider
appears, disappears
weaving the letters
of my dream into the daylight
so I remember.

Flatworld

Walking through coastal fog
the next morning
by pelicans, swans and seagulls,
a woman sweeping leaves off the pavement
as I walk towards
my usual world.

The shoes I wore when we danced
flat foot clogging
on city streets now,
heat and your music inside
the red dress I wore in your dream.

Somewhere inside a melody
called Flatworld,
I am still dancing with you,
the colors of sea anemones
speaking to me in mermaid language.

On the streetcar, a woman
holds her daughter and reads
The Tibetan Book of Living and Dying.
This is my world now, climbing
the rhythm of an Appalachian
fiddle tune.

Amazing to feel this intensity
inside my body, my womb
curving ocean moonshell
and it feels like home.

Iowa Omen

Three hawks fly south
    as your voice trembles
        across the great plains.

Fields of sleeping cows
    a gentleness in the land.

Here is the omen:
    Sky splashed with aurora,
        blue stars, curtains of light.

The letters are gold
    on red silk —
        Japanese calligraphy.

If I had the right kind of ink
    I'd write them
        on your skin.

Swan Light

DNA
Hebrew letters
I Ching

May my light awaken yours
in swan light
free from an ancient pattern, now
singing inside your cells
without restrictions.

Your body is constantly shifting
into new constellations,
breathing, awakening.
Blue water, first light, will not
be contained.

It's a pattern encrypted in language
you know inside your cells,
buffalos on the wall of the cave
dreaming in a language where
ancient letters sing.

Wake up now!
The sun is tumbling through coastal fog,
where the swans say everything —
because birds talk to you
as they talk to me
in a language older than words.

You are a musical instrument,
swan light breathing
violet
violoncello wind
through the strings.

UNCONVENTIONAL BEAUTY

Unconventional Beauty

It was amazing to see my bones
that afternoon. Shins, ankle, feet.
Unconventional beauty.
White as an ice storm.

At the contra dance,
hot fiddle music, drums,
a kaleidoscope of bodies
whizzing through colors and form.
Flying, soaring, effortless.

I remember waking up inside
a lovely piece called "The Rain."
Cello and violin, gentle and moving.
Your image as I play it.

And what was that song
called tenderness?
Music of the spring blooming.
White heron. Lavender. Swan.
But this is private.

In the place where I once lived,
the Russian olive fell
inside the echo of the elm.
Ice storms from my time in Iowa.
A glittering war zone of dead branches.

Try to let go of the pain
and keep the gift.
Tell your heart to refuse
to be broken.

Meditation on the MUNI

When you can't understand the language,
the syllables sound like birds —
old Chinese women chirping like catbirds
perched on a mulberry branch,
searching for fermented cherries.
Norwegian, a dogsled
weaving down the mountain.
Swedish, a wobbling luge.
German and Hebrew, an argument
into the wounds of the previous century.
Nepali, rocks in a river
singing under white water.
Hindi, an amber flow of chanting honey.
French, a casual flirtation
at the painted tables of a café
by the Left Bank.
Tagalog, papayas from the Philippines.
Spanish, the music of the earth.

That man with the tattooed bull's-eye
on his right leg,
a target for poison darts
blown by aboriginal tribes in the rain forest
close to the Anaconda River,
or water sports in the Castro District?
The woman with blue hair
having an argument with her lover
and everyone riding the streetcar . . .
Cell phone citation?
Too loud and way too private.
No, we don't want to know.

Second citation for leopard dress clashing
with zebra boots.

I was hoping to close my eyes
and swirl into the rushing waters
of a Himalayan River,
a turquoise ferris wheel, the dogsled
of meditation,
constellations swirling a *devanagari* riddle,
then get lost in the leopard light
of an afternoon dream
or the next chapter of a Mexican novel
in the genre of magical realism —
the one with the whole town eating
animal crackers laced with a secret
potion giving everyone erotic dreams.
What was I thinking?

Dreaming the Dragon

He presses a butterfly tattoo
on his baby's leg,
smoothing the imprint of the water.
He'd like his little one
to grow up and play the cello
or find her own way
of living close to the soul.

As I run to the N-Judah streetcar,
Jason from the Burrito Shop
holds the door for me.
I am on my way to the symphony,
and the ten minute edge of this train
will let me usher in the orchestra
instead of the balcony.

On the streetcar, we talk about Beethoven,
and the way you embrace a cello,
holding the music
close to your heart, with
the passion of your sacred fire.

He says that heavy metal is like a symphony —
it has a large sound,
and he remembers a child prodigy,
the beauty of the girl as astounding
as her virtuoso violin at Davies Symphony Hall.
Maybe his daughter will be a musician
and play there one day.
He shows me a photograph, his daughter
three weeks old, and doesn't tell me why
she is still at the hospital.

Before he leaves the streetcar
to climb the hill to the ICU,
he tells me to come to Beach Burrito
on Judah, close to the ocean, if I need anything.
Really, I mean it, he says.
I live by the edge of Golden Gate Park.
I'd like to hear you play the cello.

His eyes are so transparent
he doesn't care if a stranger is
three weeks old, thirty or eighty.
As I watch him walk up the hill to Parnassus Street,
I think about Beethoven's Seventh Symphony
and how I'm aching to play it,
but tonight, listening will be my pleasure.

After the concert, as he climbs into the music
of the fields of sleep,
I play a musical prayer for his daughter
and the dream dragon whispers —
body of a cloud, gold scales shining,
lit up from within.

Artifact

My dreams shimmer with the arrival
of ladybugs and dragonflies,
a curtain of light
in the northern sky,
night music.

Memories of a summer lake,
the ripple of a canoe on Bear Mountain.
A tiny spotted frog
in a cup,
an artifact of memory.

Two monarch butterflies
flutter in mating dance,
a wave of redwing blackbirds
lifting from the white boards
of a fence by a field of black-eyed Susans.

The blue glass bottle you buried
under the house,
an artifact to be discovered
during an archeological dig
in ten thousand years,
if our planet survives . . .

My prayer for the eucalyptus —
a single note on the cello,
lemon scented geraniums,
a hummingbird
vibrating the salty ocean air
the way music triggers memory.

Kites

Laughter floating like a kite
over ghosts of water.
Ghosts of clouds, ghosts of rivers,
ghost of who I was before
Kore carried me to the underworld.

I feel you in an airplane
flying from Wisconsin to hurricane zone,
asleep and dreaming thick branches
hurled though your house
by a dragon wind
while the roof is shaking.

I wake up early morning
with the shape of your legs around me,
body heat flying away
in the echo of a dream.

I collect potions as gifts
until you fly west again –
Fat Tire Amber, Sierra Nevada,
a story for your son
since you like these things.

In the afternoon, I go hiking by the Bay
with Kore spinning visions in the underworld —
time moving and standing still.
Gecko, dragon kite, yin-yang
floating in the sky.
Love, like the Phoenix, in the ashes
then reborn.

Black Bear Walking through her Dream

Flying out of Kentucky in a small Mesaba jet
rising above the horse farms,
white fences, tiger lilies, catalpa trees,
the Harmony Church of God.
Above Cumberland Falls, the Red River Gorge,
peppercorn cheese scones at Magee's Bakery,
wine glasses at the Bombay Brazier.
Light on the brown sway of
majestic stallions.

Last night I dreamed about a mask
breaking, a glass animal
shattering. An earthquake
ripping through the mountains,
and the house by the swans
falling down. I saw
the damage first at the altar.

Time is supposed to keep things
from slamming into each other,
but time creates too much distance.

Walking with the dog I call Needle Nose,
we climb the mountain to Echo Summit,
as a lug of a black bear
walks deeper into the winter.
In the cabin, a fire and a friend.
Fantail fish swimming through her paintings.
Sand dollars gather inside a tsunami,
with a bare-chested woman draping herself
over a crescent moon.

As I sleep, the black bear leads me
higher into the mountains,
where I fly to you on wings of joy,
a ruby-throated hummingbird lifting from the water.
Two thousand miles away, in an Appalachian forest,
you paint the umbrella magnolia
over the Red River Gorge,
your hand dipping into blue glass,
a bowl of oranges.

In the echo of your dreams,
I send you pink.
I send you divine tenderness.

Letting Go in an Earthquake Zone

It's a risk living by the water
in Earthquake Zone.

Strangers become oracles,
at concerts and street corners, predicting fog
and six months to get out of San Francisco.
Hummingbirds flutter to the balcony
in a green blur, with my soul's voice chanting,
You are the Earth.
Your body is the Earth.

Love anchors me to the heat,
the music of gravity filling with water.
In the silence between oceans,
my emotions staring at guard rails
over the bridge.

Loving is always a risk,
a dive into the unknown
without a guard rail,
a candle inside the labyrinth,
echo of my home.
A wandering into the mystery of skin,
a song inside a constellation.
Long boats from Atlantis rowing to Egypt,
a riddle path on a green table,
cutting the melon
open.

He walked into the ice floe
leaving a trail of music.

His notes were elk,
white owls, polar bears,
a geisha moon shining on his face.

And what do I want?
To honor the gift you gave me.
To bless you every night.
To release myself into the hands of angels
and float in the immensity,
singing inside an expanding sea of stars.

In the Outer Sunset

In November, I move boxes
to the Outer Sunset, and rediscover
my cello, a tambourine, a blue butterfly.
Two origami cranes folded by tiny Japanese hands,
a dream catcher with three feathers.
Feng shui   yin yang.
A carved wooden box from Bali,
my cactus and succulent garden,
a crystal snowflake.
Two baby angels kissing behind
a geisha handkerchief.

A meteor shower across the Pacific sky,
as I unroll the White Tara tanka.
Carefully, with earthquake hooks,
I hang my father's etchings on the wall,
then the Chagall green donkey
riding to the moon.
By the window, the shaman painting
of turtle island.

One by one, I release gifts from their boxes —
light from The Dreaming Room,
fortune cookie with message:
*Friends long absent are coming
back to you.*
My heart, a rose-scented candle
still burning
across the distance.

At the ocean, a storm tide —
dramatic light pushing through slate
grey clouds.
Seagulls, pelicans, osprey,
shafts of sun beaming through
clouds about to rain.

Inside the whir of my life,
a transition
pushing through dragonfly paper.
Calla lilies releasing
the fractal
into their first winter bloom.

I attach legs to carved wood —
the kitchen table from my father,
his gift, set with Japanese plates,
a bowl of cherries
and three tea candles.
Later, a simple meal of miso soup
with ginger and winter squash.

The moon, a waterfall
of light through my window.
Meteor showers, the trajectory of a star
as it burns.

On my cello, I sound the open strings,
then the Bach Prelude in G major.
Later an improvisation, my hands
filling themselves
with the shaman music I heard
before sunrise, in the fractal
of a rose-scented dream.

Ballet of the Dusty Dream

He watches himself in the mirror,
soldier's muscles turned graceful,
heart at the frantic end
of glass.

The olive leaves of his face
lost in the drumming of
the *tambour*, petals
of bougainvillea
twisting around his hands.

He kicks his left foot
high above his shoulders
before he leaps and pirouettes,
his heart escaping
from the rain and the Moroccan
ghetto of his childhood.

His heart is a fisherman.
The light escaping from his net
shatters the music
as his hips spin into ancient
Babylonian temple fire.

He arches his back
above the cobalt of the ocean
with the constellations spinning
towards the dawn.
But dawn is a fortune teller
who won't reveal her secrets.

Inside the curve of a nautilus shell,
his hips shatter the music.
Fractals of galaxies braid themselves
into the poetry of his cheekbones.
His eyes run with the
gazelles, and his heart is

gone.

What the Wind Said

In the harvest of disappointment,
life was born to break your heart.
I ask for love,
and the wind says no.
Some souls are blessed with easier paths,
family and home,
fire on a dark planet.
Sun like jewels on the river
where the turtle speaks.
The wind shatters my spirit.
My parents, tree and stone
moving toward the end of their days.
I have more time on the river,
arms a woven scarf with a golden thread
around the neck of a brown cow.
What I thought of love,
burned in the ash.
I sit on the rock,
and the river is roaring.
The wind says wake up
every morning
where the dragonfly whispers secrets.
Listen to the river.
Be open to the gift.

Staccato

She floats on the ceiling
watching the room below
out of her body
never knowing when the brick will fall.
Upstairs her parents are teaching her that marriage
is a prison, a cage, an abomination.
She plays cello to escape.
She falls asleep —
midnight eclipse, dark forest.
A message inside the oak
where the owl says,
there's always that one final
barrier at the end.

She floats on the ceiling
as her body sits on the sofa
with the boy in the recreation room.
He calls her breasts tomatoes,
wants to touch them.
She thinks this is funny,
not the proper language.
Rosebuds would be a better word.
She wonders where her parents are.

Her friends tell her to sit on a sand dune
and watch the waves
until the sun falls.
Maybe the rhythm of the ocean
will help her stop shaking.
Her parents were upstairs sleeping
when he climbed through the window.

The angel showed it to her before it happened,
told her when to be still
and when to run. She got away.

Her parents deny the memory
when the police come,
say the man could not possibly be their friend.
They say this over and over
until she cannot access her memories.
The angels scattered like stones
but maybe the timpani of green
Atlantic waves will wash her in salt
and help her remember.

Shostakovich takes her to emotions
beyond what she knew before —
a journey up the neck of the cello
above the harmonic on the A string.
Outside, the snow is piling.
She's walking in drifts up to her knees.
The court jester is pounding snowballs
at her window. Icy staccato.
It's an act, an incantation, not real.
And what does he know about love?
Wanting to be different from her parents,
she avoids alcohol, smokes marijuana.

She wants to leave the past under a snowdrift,
create a new life. She moves to California
and doesn't play cello for fifteen years.
She blows her memories
into two grey stones at the beach
and throws them into the ocean.
She can't see the future
but wants it to be different.

Before she sleeps, she asks the owl
for a message.

Shaft of light. Intuitive message.
Can't access language right now.
They keep the future hidden
under a calla lily.
Angels laugh.
They know — won't tell me.
Figure it out like music.
Discover it as you go.
We're always guiding you,
even when you don't know.
Amen.

When she plays cello again,
she does it for different reasons,
and the music reveals itself
at a deeper level,
teaches her body how to follow.
The music reveals the angel
hidden in her soul,
invites her to dance
in a world that is new
each morning.

On the other side of the continent,
she watches swans in the morning,
plays cello on the balcony
over the duck lagoon.
Love is still an enigma,
an unfinished dream, a snowball
spinning inside a hamster cage,
but the door is open now.

Maybe a message, new light
running underneath a clatter of memory.
Love is a hummingbird she holds in her hand,
feeds him drops of sugar water,
asks him to fly. A promise
where dawn comes
in a rush of white deer.

A View from the Moon

As we move into the darker time,
my friends are scattered around a globe
rocked by hurricanes and tsunamis.
Where does the soul find leaves
for its unexpressed longing
in a forest of bare trees?

I would like to believe that love
finds its way in the world.
My voice is breaking
as I push myself through the keyhole
to the shimmer of light
on the other side.

At the edge of the continent,
I find a necklace of broken pottery,
a spiral of conch,
a lacework of pelican prints
in the sand.

I search for Buddha
in a Chinatown market,
the single note that vibrates,
the moment of the vulnerable heart
where I wake up inside an Appalachian fiddle tune
in the minor key of the mountains.

There's a footprint in the sand of the soul,
before people deviate
from the path their soul has chosen.
In the crashing waves after midnight,

where does the soul
find the imprint of its longing?

In the sand I piece together
fragments of broken clay
with a desire to transmute
everything that is not holy
in a world that is still finding its form.

What we can't express
becomes the planetary nightmare.
The soul hydroplanes, slips off the road.
In the early morning moonlight,
a black spider
crawling over my leg
with its message.

But I wake up from the dream of a man
who hypnotized me
spinning
in a hot tub
and made my cello float.

I am the woman on the moon,
a crescent of possibilities
at the edge of the constellation
where night becomes morning,
Isis holding the ankh on her throne
in a robe that matches the midnight sky.
She tells me I need to start expecting
the good things to come true.

On the Earth, a depression and a hysteria —
a memory of Minoan times,

an oracle in the rock,
Arctic Wilderness
River Gorge,
a clay vessel filling with light
as my vision becomes the music
becomes the man,
and climbs into bed with me.
I want in all ways
to be a blessing.

DAWN AFTER THE ART WALK

Meditation on an Ostrich Egg

Memory is like an egg —
a strip of fog over the bridge,
cascading, rippling hills
in a waterfall.
Below the stones,
a symphony of frogs.

Balancing in my hand,
an ostrich egg
held captive in a box,
the embryo emptied through a tiny hole,
an ellipsoid eggshell universe
waiting to be painted
with a fine tipped brush.
Inside it, the memory
of a farmhouse where I don't live anymore,
not cracking. *Imagine the nest!*
Quite an omelette!

I toss things off
and he writes them down,
feels they are important.
Chrysanthemums on my kimono
fall into the Red Sea.
It's a geisha dance,
a feast of pomegranates
painted on an eggshell.

Halfway around the globe,
people believe the universe
waits inside an egg
before it is tossed to the edges
of an infinite cosmos. Further south,
below the Tropic of Capricorn,
an ostrich pushes a
hard and round universe
into a nest —
believing in the dream of birth.

Dawn after the Art Walk

Line of a train on the north side of town
an hour before sunrise.
I open the early morning window
to snow under a street lamp.
In my bedroom, a chill in the walls,
a loneliness deeper than my bones.

Changing my shoes after the waltz,
I walk into the cold air alone.
By the door to the Landmark Hotel
at exactly the wrong moment,
I witness a marriage unraveling.
In one evening, in front of me
all of the reasons I left this place.

Dreams tumble like the paintings I saw —
tree frogs splotching a red barn
under an arch of cottonwood branches,
a dancer climbing blue star stairs
to the Pleiades.

Five years ago, I packed up
what was most important to me
in my Toyota and drove
west across the mountains.
In the back seat,
my cello, my dance shoes, my favorite books
including the one I was writing.

Somewhere inside, beyond the snow
I knew about you
and knew you were not here.

Journey to an Unseen Place

A musical staff on my arm
was etched by a rosebush,
but the melody has not revealed itself.
I visit the house in Iowa
where I lived for many years,
a life dismantled and recreated
differently, somewhere else.

Deeper into the winter,
I fly over Appalachian Mountains,
watch the sun setting over Manhattan,
the arch of the Verrazano Narrows Bridge,
a stripe of pink between sky and water.
Gazing out of a fifth floor window
over the Hudson River,
I wonder what I will dream here.

My visions fly further west,
yellow flowers growing through rocks,
ponderosa pines, cerulean sky.
On the streetcar, a girl from China
sits next to me and sings
all the way
to the Outer Sunset.

With each sunrise,
I recreate my life, stretching myself
where I have not traveled before,
trusting the deeper journey
and the truth which reveals itself
from the body and the heart.

With each sunrise,
I let the world be new
as I swim through the illusion
of ice in winter water.
Music brings memory, heat, a vision
I discover as it sings.

Isis Initiation

Two deer running into a meadow
beyond the cottonwood tree.
A herd of cows before sunset
by the red barn on Pleasant Plain Road.
I return to the house where I planted tiger lilies
in the garden by my window.
Pleiades and the Scorpion in the sky.
So good to see the stars again.

My house welcomes me back —
Buddha, turtles, mani stones
from Nepal. A sunflower
in the altar of my garden
by tangles of blackberry vines.
A final bloom of tomatoes.

Two thousand miles away,
you are playing Brahms on the cello.
A bass tremolo cadence
in a minor key
travels through the night sky.
Above me, northern constellations
through Russian olive branches.

Ladybugs on the ceiling
lead me deeper into a dream
of dragonflies and glass angels.
I polish silver candlesticks
with memories of my grandmothers.
Inside the pyramids, an ancient promise.

Peacock feathers, a band of gold
around his head and mine.
My grandmother's voice as I
hear her whisper.

Dreams cross distances,
a stripe of light over the water
into the open sky, a musical prayer.
He stirs his visions in a blue bowl,
kneads them like bread,
a swirl of silver, an initiation —
Tibetan tankas pouring light into the altar
of the open heart.

Prom Night in Fairfield, Iowa

A wave of spotlights lures everyone to the glitter
an hour before midnight,
as dancers empty out of the gym
and drive around the town square
in a parade of vintage cars.

The prom queen,
decorated like a castle of cotton candy,
waves and throws Hershey's kisses
from the cabin of her grandfather's John Deere tractor.
Cheerleaders wave their pom-poms
above the chrome of old convertibles,
while the captain of the football team
tosses Mardi Gras necklaces from the front seat
of a pink bubbleback Barracuda.

The girls' basketball team
stands on the running boards of a Power Wagon,
while their younger sisters follow
waving kisses from the windows
of a two-tone Rambler
redesigned as an art car.

As they drive around the town square,
they are illuminated with spotlights
as bright as the evening Uncle Henry's Bonneville
made its debut at the Pontiac showroom.
They are glass swans, ephemeral sculptures,
princess and frog,
carrying a glitter-bag of dreams.

Each couple is announced
as they leave their chrome chariots,
and walk the white carpet to show
swanky satin gowns and bare shoulders.

We sit in the bleachers
as they sashay into the dance hall
above the Elk's Lodge
for a pizza party,
and I wonder if wishes alone
can make these girls so voluptuous.

No exit to the haystacks.
Every high school Juliet
is chaperoned from dusk to dawn.
The Co-ed Theatre opens at 2 a.m.
for a showing of *Gone with the Wind*.

The Red Door

Late at night, he plays Vivaldi and Tchaikovsky.
It comes from an intense privacy.
Years ago, he was the Fiddler on the Roof.
Now he refuses to play for anyone
but himself.

Sometimes he lets his father listen
through the door. Images of
the police separating his parents.
Fire and water filling the house.

In Iowa, winter is rolling across the great plains.
A chill in the morning, frost on blackberry vines.
Late at night, the place where my shoulder aches.
Tears like music falling for
the honeybee, the polar bear.

Dreams of a river of music
as I fly west again
back to the trajectory
of a cello chanting prayers,
the Tibetan prayer shawl
I wrap around his shoulders.

Ode to Egg Yolk

Three-legged scaredy-kitty
limping like a broken
egg yolk
with a mangy coat.

The broken toe
of our neighborhood,
butt end of a bad joke
that keeps echoing
on the roof at midnight.

You attempted to bring your fleas
into our house
as you lunged for comfort,
wanting to make your new bed
on our red welcome mat
during a house concert.

I watched you burrowing
into the hedge below the passion flowers
and the Pacific sky,
hoping to surprise a hummingbird,
a parakeet or a tanager.

In your nest of overheated
sere summer grass,
you dream of a past life as a soldier
wounded in the Civil War,
resting by a fire on a bed of rags.

You startle as I approach you,
scuttle away from the garbage can,
yowling from the fence top
with your lucky leg dragging,
stalking the neighborhood skunk
around the corner.

Last Day in Iowa

contrails on the way to Iowa City
horses, cows, a pig
fallow field after late autumn harvest
leaves falling from the sudden cold

barn swallows lifting up from the road
two redwing blackbirds in the hedgerow
by the tornado ditch

field of alfalfa plowed under
herd of goats on the other side
of a white crossbeam fence

red Amish barn with a hood and a hex sign
dappled field of dairy cows
dirt road between 19th century farmhouses

county road to Swisher and Shueyville
exit to the Amana Colonies
corridor of flags at the airport
echo of red twin silos

the red rose from my garden bloomed
for eight days, spreading scented light
through my kitchen window
during my pilgrimage home

Stripes of Light on their Bodies

Through Venetian blinds
stripes of light
on an arm, a leg, an echo
a lithe twisting of bodies
shining in the half
moonlight.

At one o'clock in the morning,
a light rain in Kentucky,
a motorcycle
blasting through the echo
of an open window
under emerging branches
of a catalpa tree.

Inside the window
illumination
of intertwining fingers
a twisting, a lifting, a dance
under papaya
stripes of moonlight,
a memory of a swan
charcoal pencil tracing
the tenderness of a shoulder
the soft touch of your
fingertips.

Halfway up the Mountain

Semen smells like trees
a wandering into branches
red and yellow leaves
imprint of a columbine
cadence of a new language
swimming with light.

I want to love you in the mountains
the bark of Jeffrey pines
the scent of you.

RING OF FIRE

Floating Redwoods in the Early Morning

after the eclipse sings

after the crab nebula spins a supernova in my heart
after the memories
after the brilliant starry sky
constellations whispering like runes in a cryptic language

after one day maybe next week
after ice storms wrapping trees
after the stairs lead to blessings as well as sorrow

after the cellos harmonize to the prayer you used to sing
after the floating music of the waves
after the only conversation is to enjoy your own happiness

after your parents float through the tangible horizon
and their spirits have become part of you

because our lives are essentially a mystery —
floating redwoods in the early morning
and I have never been good with goodbyes

after the night kept getting foggier and foggier
and she flew through the corona of a distant sun

after she appeared in a lucid dream
singing the old folk melodies
as fires burned redwood trees,
releasing their seeds for the next generation.

Ring of Fire

At the edge of the continent,
fires are everywhere.
Lightning strike at Point Arena.
Then a wide band of fire
traveling northeast on a summer wind.
Hundreds of lightning strikes
inside a ring of fire
torching the solstice night.

In the Mendocino Woodlands,
echoes of stellar jays,
a family of pheasants,
a mountain lion stalking in the meadow.
In the distance, burning mountains.
Images of the enigma
weaving themselves together
inside a larger vision.

For some reason I don't understand,
my mother decided to walk
back from the edge —
unable to leap at this time
through the ring of fire.

This is for my mother,
the older version of the three-year-old
who stood on the piano bench
and belted out radio tunes
and folk songs from the old country
when her relatives said in Yiddish,
Sing Mamale, Sing Little Mama.

Somewhere
in the middle of the continent
peonies in full bloom
now filling the still warm nights
with their sticky fragrance.

Somewhere
while the rest of us are
still dreaming,
a meeting with her Guardian Angels,
planning how long she will stay
and the next adventure on her soul's journey.

Mamale,
you'll probably burn a path of fire
through the sky on your way,
and wherever the meteorites and snow angels
take you next,
I hope it is glorious!

In the middle of the redwood forest,
I feel you singing
inside the spirit of the trees.

Moonbird

Walking the streets of Jacksonville
close to midnight
after Tropical Storm Fay
moves out to the gulf,
flooding and a litter of fallen
branches at our feet.

One week ago,
we were driving up the Pacific Coast
close to Mt. Shasta
in the pass between the coastal range
and the Sierras
when we received news
of her passing.

Peacefully, I am told,
and alone
rising above her broken body.

In the silent embrace of mountains
a flood of moonlight
a lacework of stars
the echo of her voice.

Sunbird
                Moonbird
                                Starbird

She flew out
through a corona of sunlight
but not the sun I know.

Circle of Stones

In the ICU, while he was dreaming
in that space-time portal between the worlds,
he must have heard the chanting
and felt deep notes resonating on the cello.
When we sang to him and played the First Bach Prelude,
I know it made him happy in his soul.

Then a single note
where the wind whispers,
he's not in this world anymore.

But the earth remembers
the red farmhouse surrounded by sunflowers,
the one lane road through the oaks,
the pond and the early green
of the earth in springtime.

Memories unfurl like a calla lily,
and it all comes back to him —
wisdom retrieved from papyrus
burned in the Alexandrian fire,
the way things done in the dark
show up in the light again.

I am singing inside a
circle of stones in the breaking dawn
at the edge of a tsunami.
Images of the Dead Sea, otherworldly.
An arc of candles leading to a star,
a child king in an Egyptian tomb.

I go to the river to swim
and rinse death
out of my black skirt.

He understands the separation between the worlds,
hard questions, difficult choices, what the soul knows.
A red rose waiting on brick stairs,
sunlight shining through red petals,
almost otherworldly.

I wish you peaceful dreams tonight —
blue stones, high cliffs, salt seas,
the caves at *Rosh Hanikra*
where the sky echoes.

You are the blessing
and you are the blessed.

In Provincetown

For Barbara Rushmore

She said that love
is the face of God.

Or maybe love is a gypsy moth
fluttering her wings,
not understanding
that she is pushing against
a window.

In her house on the bay,
we stood by the window —
deck holding against
the storm, the sand, the water.

We talked about the way
early evening light
shrinks in the fall,
rain falling on the sail of a fishing boat
floating in her kitchen,
and time goes dark,
the way
a dream light flickers.

She shared memories of my father,
the kindness in his words. Skates on the river,
the pipe they broke open with small stones,
and the house their families shared
during the Great Depression.
As we walked in the late afternoon,
she showed me where she planted a thousand trees —
Carpathian walnuts, Bradford pears, Chinese Scholar japonicas,

with origami cranes whispering in the leaves
at the tip of Cape Cod.

I remember clearly
her words of wisdom
written in the dark,
where an oak leaf on the pavement
laced by shadows
flips over
like a suddenly remembered
dream.

Late August

Late August in the garden,
a final bloom of lilies
composting an echo, an angel, a dream.

Tangerine sunset over the Pacific.
My tomatoes are still laughing at me
for trying to make them grow in the coastal fog.

My stepmother has forgotten my name,
but I hope she is still dreaming of my father
waiting for her with an embrace
of starlight.

Meteor showers fall over the mountains.
After the dance tonight
ephemeral flash of light across the sky,
tiny burning.

My grandmothers stare at me
through an open window,
Andrew Wyeth curtain blowing out to the stars
as if the ancestors wait to extend their hands
and pull her up to the spirit world.

Fold the sorrow like a flag
and give it to the sun to burn.

Under the Dogwood Tree

For Irene Frank

When I was ten years old,
my father and I planted a dogwood tree
for you on Mother's Day.
I remember our trip to the nursery
in my father's red Triumph,
and how it rode so close to the ground.
We put the top down,
to bring home the dogwood
in the back seat,
pink blossoms in a scented wind.

Every spring, the dogwood
grew and bloomed, the way I did.
It was mysterious to me
the way you loved that tree,
and you showed me something about life
I continue to plant in my garden.

As I write these words to you,
I'm watching the Pacific Ocean with the early
evening sun ready to fall into the waves
and light up the sky
pink as a blossom.
I can still hear you singing.
Hummingbirds and hibiscus in the yard,
your face in an ocean wave,
your smile and your music filling my house
in memory,
like a scented wind.

In a Jasmine Wind

For Don Frank

My father loved red.
He loved little red sports cars,
red socks and red shirts.
I had a redwood tree
planted in his honor.
I'd like to think he's a rainbow now
with a jasmine wind
floating through the garden
where every flower has his name.

I remember his Lionel trains,
our basement full of meters and test equipment,
cathode ray tubes and rainbow spaghetti wires,
and the way he carried me on his shoulders in the snow.
I remember when I was nine years old
watching him cross the stage to get his diploma
at Newark College of Engineering,
how proud I was, with my crepe paper diploma doll,
and the party that night
at Grandma Helen and Grandpa Frank's apartment
before they moved back to the farm.

I remember when he took us to Washington, D.C.
to put flowers on Kennedy's grave
and visit the tomb of the unknown soldier.
David was still so small
Dad had to hold him tight to keep him
from flying away in a fierce November wind.
While my Mom took the elevator with my brothers,
my father walked with me up thousands of steps
to the top of the Washington Monument.

I remember the way my father talked with me
about what I was learning in school
and conversed with me in the Spanish
he learned in the Merchant Marines.
I loved his ship stories —
the captain whose hair turned white,
what he did while docked in India,
Spain, the Panama Canal,
New Orleans and the open sea.
Yes, I heard the subtext —
get educated, travel and see the world
before you even think of getting married.

The first time I met Edie,
they took me to dinner at The Meeting Place
where they discovered each other
and he insisted that she start dating again.
As our waiter served the shrimp scampi,
Dad went after Edie's nose with a pair of chopsticks.
That evening was the first time I heard
his favorite toast, often repeated
during almost thirty years of marriage,
"May you be as happy as we are."

I like to think of my father sitting in the sunshine,
perhaps on a park bench in another world,
light within him, light all around him,
light showering on him
like a sky full of shooting stars.
I know he is at peace and happy,
catching up on things, reading the book of life,
and enjoying the view.

I like to think that he was finally
able to see Erik on Sunday,

his blue eyes and wild curly hair,
while we were waltzing
at Meike and James' wedding dance.

I like to think that every night,
Edie can visit with him while she is dreaming
and hear him whisper
the last words he said in this body,
"I love you. I love you. I love you."

And to you, my dear father,
we wish you

Peace in your body.
Peace in your soul.

Fly free. Fly with love.
Fly with the angels.

Embraced by the mountain,
final flight.

Love returning to love.
Light returning to light.

Message from Another World

Her voice came from winter:
the earth turning on its axis,
the sun lower on the horizon,
setting earlier, between Venus and the Pole Star.
The first snow showers of the season
early in the morning.

Losing your Mama is large and mysterious —
a powerful initiation.   Traces of shooting stars
inside the silk cocoon of the heart,
a descant of honeybees,
a journey that takes you even deeper
into the Wise Woman
because you have to find her voice
inside yourself.

Inside the swirling snow,
a melody weaves through
the ruby necklace your grandma wore,
a canon in a star of dreams
with a missing note in the chord.
It's the voice of your mother,
and you have to burrow like a chipmunk
under the snow
to hear her singing.

I remember those times in Iowa
after the cottonwood dropped its leaves,
snow floating under a street lamp,
then the aurora at the northern border.

Winter has a stark beauty,
but the coldness always went inside.

Ice shimmering branches
as they pull to the silent earth,
images like jewels,
and I feel them glow between the worlds.

Wolf Moon

For Edie

His wife was fiercely loving
during the final days of my father's life.
She was a moon rising over the ocean
illumined with an inner light
recovering a lucidity
we had not seen in many years.

A woman warrior, trying to pull him back
from the underworld.

Above the coastal mountains
a vision of the wolf moon —
craters and penumbra.
The ellipsis of a twin soul rising
in sparks of initiation.
The veil between the worlds lifted
as the largest moon of the year orbits
closest to earth.

Her eyes are full of night whispers,
the Milky Way, tumbling through the sky
clouds like cliffs with white waves
illumined by an inner light.

Requiem

For Edie

The door opens on Tuesday.
On Friday she walks away from the world.
I saw them at the Symphony,
Brahms and one hundred voices around them.
He was wearing a black suit with a top hat,
she in a long silk evening gown,
his arm softly around her shoulder.
They waved at me from a high window
and then they walked into the stars.

Nobody else could see them
but they waved at me
from a high box in the air.
In the fortissimo,
low pedal tones of the organ
vibrated the ceiling and the walls,
and in the quiet moments
one hundred voices hummed
the chord of the earth
as it turned.

In another world,
she is skating on a river
in the rose pink of sunset or dawn.
A fox fur hat around her face
keeps her warm, sheltering her
as a cottonwood tree from thunder.
These memories comfort as a soft pillow,
green and cool, a meadow
glowing with wild irises and daffodils,
the path through the forest where you walked,
where the leaves of your life
glow like rhapsodies at your feet.

Seven Visions of My Mother

1. Wax Angel

Seven voices of my mother
singing above the mountains,
wing of a message etched
by a seven day candle.

Her voice
blesses the fire by the ocean
the apples in my kitchen
the music I play.

She sings to me every morning
from the classical radio station,
on KJazz through the jay blue sky,
first voice of the robin
through the f-hole of my cello.

2. Provincetown

Mamale sings to my friends
in their dreams, blesses their visions,
tells me to keep dancing.

I think of my Cousin Barbara
digging oysters in Provincetown
from the harbor by the Bay.
She rents the big house
during the sunny time of the year.
Mamale swam with her
in the salty water.

With a canvas of sky, clouds and memory,
Mamale is painting chords of ocean,

the music of her soul,
wooden boats with white sails,
and a huge blue sky.

In a telephone call, Barbara tells me,
She was so proud of you.
You were everything
she wanted a daughter to be.

3. Cello Duets

Erik and I played cello for her
a transposed duet
of the Hebrew prayer
she used to sing with her closest friend,
who escaped from Berlin as a girl
after *Kristallnacht.*

He played "May the Words" as a quartet
with two violins and a viola
in the middle of a redwood forest,
his cello singing to her
through redwood trees.

We were in the Mendocino Woodlands.
Each day I called for a message.

My last words to her . . .
A poem. Ring of Fire.
I love you so much, Mama.
You know how much I love you.

Her last words to me . . .
You should keep him.

4. By the Ocean

We were both convinced
Mamale was working behind the scenes
to help us find our home by the ocean.
She wanted me to have the fireplace,
huge windows, flocks of seagulls,
waves of inspiration.

We moved book cases, desks and a dresser
on top of a Mazda Protege,
with camping pads, rope, and bungee cords.
It was totally hilarious — should have been a movie
to share with friends, especially the bed
on top of the Mazda.

There are pieces of my family all over the house —
silver candlesticks from my great-grandmother,
my grandma's silver sugar and creamer,
my mother's jewelry, her *menorah*.
Quan Yin, Buddha, Krishna,
family photographs,
a birthing Goddess from Africa
art deco lamps from Italy
with an angel playing the flute.

5. Davies Symphony Hall

It was amazing to be on the same stage
as my teacher, playing Handel's *Messiah*
at Davies Symphony Hall.
The stage has tremendous energy
from all of the musical souls
through the years playing music there.

Looking out to the second tier
was at first overwhelming,
but with some coaching and calming
from my friend who plays the flute,
I was able to immerse myself in the music
and play with passion and joy.

During the second part of the concert,
my knees starting shaking
during a pianissimo
where the cellos were exposed.
That is exactly when I felt
my mother's hand on my back,
my Mama, who could fill a concert hall
without a microphone,
now filling me,
and the rest of the concert was pure joy.

6.   Message from the Snow

My friend calls from the snow of Vermont.
Ice storm to ocean.

The Wise Woman is speaking . . .
Have you noticed how the two of us
have been on a similar journey for several months now,
how the Wise Woman goes deeper
after your mother enters the spirit world?

For the first two months,
I needed a lot of time to be quiet
and the world didn't pull me with its quiet tide.
But when I emerged from that cave,
I had something more powerful
to give back to the world.

My Mama has ways of letting me know
she loves me. A dream,
an angel, a feather from the sky.
A letter falls out of a box . . .
I'm thinking of you today
and your beautiful smile.
Love, Mom.

7. Up There

It's early morning.
I feel her in the shower,
hear her voice in the walls of my house
by the edge of the continent,
see her shining smile in the silver
of my great-grandmother's sabbath candlesticks.

I hear her music
in every note I play on the cello,
in every ocean wave,
in the flamingo pink of the sunrise
every morning —
Jupiter shining over the ocean,
the moon tilted towards the Sea of Tranquility.

I've been told she's up there
on concert tour,
leaning against the mahogany of a grand piano
singing her heart's joy
with the musical saints of her generation —
Count Basie, Duke Ellington, Danny Kaye.
Harmonies are different there,
a multidimensional rainbow of
conception, invention, innovation,
the music of the soul
with freedom as immense as the night sky.

Unveiling

Today, the morning
of my father's one year candle,
my emotions,
a second year orchid,
a lavender circle of memories blooming.

In the city of the dead,
my father comes to a window
to gaze
at the ones he loves.

In the apartment where they lived,
filled with etchings,
his wife sitting on the sofa
and she doesn't know
his arms are around her.

His granddaughters
splashing around the pool in their yard
over the canyon.
David at the controls of a CAD/CAM machine,
creating the wing of a huge plane.
Lydia making a *ristofel* in the kitchen.

Ron and Eileen hiking in Carmel
with binoculars and a bird book.
Erik in Florida
getting ready to haul
the rest of his earthly possessions
to San Francisco in his red Volvo wagon
with a Mustang five-liter engine.

Today,
not an overwhelming sadness
but something like the Bach Sarabande
from the Second Unaccompanied Cello Suite
filling the room.

In the afternoon,
I plant eighteen marigolds
and other beauties
by the side of our home,
in the Don Frank Memorial Garden.

On the other side of the city,
a man who walked here from Mexico
sells strawberries and papayas
on the corner of Monterey.

At the edge of the continent,
the ocean dramatic
and now a storm
gathering
over the Pacific.

And life on this planet,
spinning like a cat's-eye marble,
wakes up with the sun
and continues.

FIRST LIGHT

Coda to a Transformation

Time has become a stranger
walking barefoot into the light.
You think about sunlight through a forest
of redwood trees, a diamond under the weight
of a hidden river, the thousand ways
your life becomes your face.

After seven seasons,
your parents become your memory,
a legacy of ghosts.
They give you an ankh
and a torch to hold.
Blue flame. Mysterious music.
A tamboura from the afterlife.
Your face becomes your memory,
fiercely loving.

You're still trying to remember
the message that flashed and disappeared
from the chalkboard. A blue feather.
A copper penny on the pavement.
A window where a face
appeared and disappeared.

What was that singing from the other world?
Voices in the morning
as you gather mint and arugula
from your garden by the ocean. Salty air.
You're trying to reinvent yourself.
The feathers tell you

the message will not appear again
in the same way,
but you need to remember.

Riding a bicycle to a memory
in Washington Heights,
the street curving up to a
total eclipse of the moon,
the hymn of a nightingale,
the birth of a galaxy
flying out of a sea of first light,
you meet yourself in the middle
of opposite directions.

You're wanting to be brilliant
as you walk into the rain,
but further inside the supernova
of your own blossoming heart,
a deeper vision is whispering,
letting you throw
whatever stops you from dancing
into the fire.

Butterflies

In Ms. Matsumoto's home living class,
we learned to sit with our legs crossed.
In fishnet stockings, red sandals and miniskirts,
our salon of budding seventh grade girls
learned her version of ladylike manners.
On her clutch of neatly arranged
Japanese sofas and chairs,
we learned to converse like geishas.
We served small trays of hors d'oeuvres —
crackers with cheese and pickles arranged in a trident,
and learned to eat them slowly.
Under her tutelage, I developed a lifelong
love of the Triscuit.

We constructed gingham aprons
and were forced to baste every stitch
even though I already knew how to use
the Singer machine at home.
Everything took twice as long as my attention span.
I didn't learn to sew anything I would wear
until my Grandma helped me
with a circle skirt
printed with pictures of musical instruments.

We were all butterflies
circling the halls of our education,
but I am convinced that no one learns manners
until her shining star
has circled around the sun many times.
A girl in seventh grade does not know

how her actions knock against the world
and ricochet into the fractal
of human feelings. Or how a joyful word
can make a stranger smile for the next ten years.
We wore tight jeans, purple suede jackets
and rainbow scarves cascading to our knees.
A girl in seventh grade does not know
the power of her heartbreaking beauty.

Betty

In your kitchen of overfed cats
and oversized mugs of tea,
you taught me how to hug.
My family was unraveling,
but your door was always open
and your hugs warmed the earthquake.

Your daughter was one of my closest friends,
part of a self-named circle called
"Friends for Life."
We walked on the golf course behind your house,
got high, harmonized Peter, Paul and Mary
with Patty's Martin guitar.
In the Adirondacks, we went camping
under spruce, pine and broad-leafed trees,
and built illegal fires, playing with our shadows
under the moonlight.

Mu tea was a religion,
and Pinchot Falls was our cathedral.
Our sanctuary of friends
met in the forest under night trees.
With my February birthday
catapulting me beyond the 21-year mark,
I bought the Isabel Rose
we hid under our jackets at the movies.

As we wandered our separate paths
on the long maze to adult life,
the threads that connected
the "Friends for Life"
grew thin. We had our occasional

visits by the Pacific Ocean,
holidays in New Jersey or Connecticut.
When your daughter became a mother,
she didn't know I could still
understand her life.

When I saw you just a month ago,
delivered to your doorstep by your doctor,
I didn't know that our hug
would be our last. You gave me
another huge cup of tea,
asked me to water your plants.
Together, we called your daughter,
and when it was my turn,
we talked for a long time.

Last week I heard the details
of your last labored breathing,
and how the air ran out.
As you told your family you were
leaving this world,
I was on the other side of the continent.
I so much wanted to be there
when they brought your ashes through the forest
close to High Point
and let what was left of you
scatter in the wind.

Since that moment, I have thought of you so many times,
your whisper, an unexpected voice
in the shower, an intuition,
a blessing from a stranger with a smile
that reminds me of your face.
The comfort in a cup of tea,

a branch of wisteria, with the leaves
curling around the music
your granddaughter plays on the cello.
Even as you were leaving this world,
I felt you in the waterfall,
your arms like water now,
your laughter, shimmering in the voice
of your daughter.

Pieces of December

Started to learn the Vivaldi
concerto for two cellos
in G minor.

My method:
listen over and over to
Yo-Yo Ma playing Vivaldi,
then aim for the impossible.

Planted a dozen iris bulbs
in the sandy soil,
arugula, sorrel and winter lettuce
in the garden.

Liberated rosemary, lavender and the fence
from the strangle hold of
passion flower vines.
No, passion should not
choke.

Hair curling in San Francisco humidity
between winter storms,
fractals of calla lilies
opening in a light rain.

Yes, I know
we don't own this house
and one day will move from here,
but I don't believe that anyone owns the earth,
though at times we are given
small pieces to care for.

Spiralesque

For McCoy Tyner

A spiral, a hissing snake,
a cadence of uprising music.
A winding sunbeam, a windmill.
A spiral is what you don't
want an airplane to do.

The geography of a joke
weaves a squiggle, the flash of a firefly,
an extended chord weaving into
pieces of laughter.
The squiggle swirls into a shivering
cloud, a snake
shimmering out from under a rock.

A square is a hard day, a mathematical riddle,
a self-absorbed clown telling an off-color joke.
A square is a bad dream
with scaly wings and coiled mouthparts
as dawn shivers over a mountain.

A leaf shivers in the path
of a bumblebee's fuzzy flight.
The shimmering of a fritillary butterfly,
wings flashing like sunspots
on the leaf of a catalpa tree in Kentucky,
leaning over the Red River Gorge.

An octagon chases an octopus,
a bar of soap, a joke in a mathematician's dream.
An octagon crashes into a cadence
of blazing starlight —

a cone, a beam of light, a black hole,
a time warp
into a disappearing universe,
revealing a secret whisper of wind,
the light inside a stone.

The whisper of the earth
reveals a dream with fritillary wings —
a circle inside the wisdom of an orbit,
a pure white egg, a fractal of a snowflake
as it discovers its form.
The heart is an ocean, a moonlit shadow
of catalpa leaves
dancing to the door of a sea of amber dreams.

Blue Plates

blue plates for breakfast
a loaf of sourdough bread
double cream brie

echo of a waltz
two voices in cello
harmony, gypsy moth
orbiting the flame

plane flew
to Jacksonville this morning
blue voices singing
clashy, atonal, tone poem

in the wide
night of the ocean
waves of moon pulling
pizzicato of blue and green

two weeks later
echo returns in a flood
raspberry key lime harmony

Flying Home

For Joyce Sandra Uhlir

She flies on the back of a snowy owl,
a mother bird. She had no fear
as she ascended. I felt her soaring
between the stars in the belt of Orion.

Her friends tell me they are sure
she's already caught her limit of fish,
driven a golf ball down the fairway,
and enriched the spirits surrounding her.

I see her walking through fields of gold,
and I know the light is amazing
as colors are revealed
with more subtlety and warmth
than the earth tones in a redwood forest.

Down here, life continues —
stir-frying a pan full of mushrooms for soup.
On the radio, Brahms' First Cello Sonata.
The cello leads me to a realm of first light,
mysterious light
as Joyce would call it.

In the back of the house,
Erik cuts wood for a xylophone.
It's mysterious the way the note tempers
as he carves away thin layers
of rosewood with a bandsaw,
then sands the edges
to bring out the overtones.

I put on the fish lure earrings
she gave me last summer,
as Erik works a wood called Purpleheart
into music for young children.

As the days pass, Joyce will continue to fly
with the ospreys, cedar waxwings and angel birds.
On the patio of a Montessori school across the bay,
a group of five and six-year-old musicians
will fill the early afternoon
with a rosewood and Purpleheart
cacophony — early music,
notes they can follow to discover
what sings in their lives.

Yahrzeit

As my acupuncturist pointed out yesterday,
the old rituals were created by someone a long time ago
because they helped them. They may or may not help me.
My mother would have preferred to take me shopping
to share her love of color and beautiful things.
So after Amy pulled the needles out
and gave me herbs that tasted like drinking a forest,
I took the streetcar to "Out of the Closet"
and took home a long leopard skirt,
a black velvet jacquard top from Banana Republic
and a black sweater woven with gold thread.
Later, Erik and I rode the cable car to Fisherman's Wharf,
pretended to be tourists, had clam chowder for dinner
and went to Pier 39 to visit the sea lions,
which are always hilarious.
Yes, I needed to laugh.

What I would have preferred to do
instead of chanting old prayers —
Play her favorite prayer on the cello.
Turn up my CD with her voice
and fill the house with her singing.
Light candles all over the house.
Send wishes to her Guardian Angels.
Fill the *yahrzeit* candle cup with wine
and rejoice that she continues to love and bless me.

I remember Inuit Grandmothers on the tundra,
chanting in mukluks, a tune called *Polar Bear Shuffle* —
a tribal dance where you can feel the weight
of bears walking through the snow.

From somewhere I don't completely understand,
I hear a waltz called *Mama's Igloo* —
still in arctic time,
igloo because they are warm inside
and full of light, like my Mama.
I dream the harmonies in her voice,
with a triple-time melody called Mama's Candle,
a hauntingly beautiful waltz in a minor key.

I know my Mama is up there dreaming stars.
I hear her voice in the waves at night
and see her in the full moon on the water.
She is whispering intuition in my dreams
and sharing the secrets of harmony
in symbols we can wonder about in the morning.

Next year, I'm going to say *kaddish*,
as promised, but the rest of it
will be a ritual I create
out of music, candles, starlight,
dancing and dreams.
Each year I'll collect more candles
until the whole house fills with light.
I want to be happy to remember her,
not unbearably sad that she is gone.

Dreams of the North

Washington Square Park
twenty years ago.
I am watching the snow beginning to pile up on the skylights.
It's too dark to watch the ice on the lake.

There's a muse inside the blizzard.
The spirit of the snow has a secret to tell you.
You might hear it in a dream.

We always went outside in ferocious storms.
We did it so that we could see and hear things
that people normally don't —
deconstructed metal, the ghost of a small animal,
silent and mysterious.

As night turns into morning,
a glitter of sun through ice-frosted branches,
red squirrels making muffled tracks,
padding across a field of emerging light.
The memory of an acorn. The deconstruction of a dream.

By the fireplace in a house circled by windows,
my heart felt like a rainbow.
I wondered if the floor would catch on fire.

Sometimes love is oblique,
from an unexpected angle, a slant of light.
Snow is falling in memory now.

Time Travel through a Convergence of Harmonics

No trees in the forest —
intergalactic cosmic dust
escaping a drift of asteroids,
later to be attacked by a space monster
in a gallery of dripping rain.

Grasshoppers in a space capsule
on a journey through time —
testament of breath
dawn of a universe
after the cosmic egg collapses
into a drift of asteroids.

Two poets sharing a pink pen
on a red table
held up by a blue egg
drifting over an asteroid
of notes and noise,
time travel into the vortex
of midnight rain.

What is the Sound of an Island?

A millennium of coral
angel skin pink
resting upon the eardrums

full of ocean,
with a cello singing in the distance,
somewhere between memory and the soul.

Billions of blue barnacles
in a galaxy of voices.

Mermaid Initiation

Follow the ribbon of twilight,
then an electric sky
at the edge of salty water.

Fish scales, a trout swimming upriver, gills
where the animal meets the angel,
a silver line of fins.

She swims in an ocean phosphorescent
with rose light, shimmering like her skin
after hours of loving.

Silver waves
awaken an inner light
as she remembers the trajectory

and the promise
of the shining ones,
whispered before the flood

before the fire, before the rain —
voices of swimming lanterns
breathing under water.

To Aphrodite

She swims in a sunrise
of amethyst light
reaching for the transparent.

Her shadow ripples through green water
where she has become
a water lily,

a forest of aspens dancing,
back arcing
into a choreography of branches.

Perseid meteor showers at night
a stripe of light over the water,
a path of silver.

She thought she was a tree
or a lichen, a tribal dance, an awakening,
a dream that rhythms can heal.

He played the lyre for her,
a touch, a sliding
that rippled through her body

and when he entered
the holy fire in the shrine of her sacred roses,
the world lit up with their singing.

Waltz for Young Daughters

In the rocking chair of a dream,
white lace ribbons of memory.
A waltz for young daughters,
aspen leaves shimmering in
the shoulder of the wind.

Open the edges of your body
to the wings of a floating swan.
Collision of a blue star
with the grace of an angel.

On the cello, even playing the scales
sounds like honey, as you weave a new song
on your grandmother's loom.
The attic is filled with boxes of old lace,
light slanting from a high window,
netting and roses on hats
from an earlier century.

Heirloom roses unfold their petals
in the garden,
pink as the cadence of your singing.
Open the painted boxes, carry the yellow silk
of your ribbons into a blooming world.
Fill the new century
with the shimmering of your dreams.

To a Hummingbird

Hummingbirds sip passion flowers
in a world lit with beauty,
green iridescent light shimmering
around their soft feathers
in the morning's first light.
The ancestors have descended to bone,
but their spirit sparkles in the world
of flying stars.   A promise
inside the light of the petals
of a yellow rose.

Come to the place
where the ocean crashes against the night
after traveling thousands of miles
in a world of dream.
Listen to the visions that whisper
inside the ripple of morning,
passion flowering inside the cadence
of every warbling songbird.

The spirit of the wise ones
who have walked this planet for millions of years
awaken in every flower,
calling your name to listen
to the song you remember
where memory whispers
and shimmers in the light.
Wake up now, singing inside
each moment of beauty.

ABOUT THE AUTHOR

Diane Frank is an award-winning poet and author of six books of poems, including *Swan Light*, *Entering the Word Temple* and *The Winter Life of Shooting Stars*. Her friends describe her as a harem of seven women in one very small body. She lives in San Francisco, where she dances, plays cello, and creates her life as an art form. Diane teaches at San Francisco State University and Dominican University. She leads workshops for young writers as a Poet in the School and directs the Blue Light Press On-line Poetry Workshop. She is also a documentary scriptwriter with expertise in Eastern and sacred art. *Blackberries in the Dream House*, her first novel, won the Chelson Award for Fiction and was nominated for the Pulitzer Prize. *Yoga of the Impossible*, her new novel, will be published soon.

To schedule readings, book signings and workshops, and to invite her to speak to your book club, contact:

E-mail: GeishaPoet@aol.com
Website: www.dianefrank.net

BOOKS BY DIANE FRANK

Yoga of the Impossible

Swan Light

Blackberries in the Dream House

Entering the Word Temple

The Winter Life of Shooting Stars

The All Night Yemenite Café

Rhododendron Shedding Its Skin

Isis: Poems by Diane Frank

Printed in the United States of America

www.ingramcontent.com/pod-product-compliance
Lightning Source LLC
Chambersburg PA
CBHW031901090426
42741CB00005B/593